In *Orvieto*, Paul Willis's entreaty to be made "more than a tourist, at least for a day" has, happily for the reader, been granted. Whether it's the "spoked halo as big and strong / as a steering wheel on a UPS delivery truck" or the play of light on distant fields that the poet and his companion "didn't know was a picture until we saw it," the observations in these dexterous, intimate poems startle me awake. They take me to Italy and, at the same time, more deeply into the "bones and blossoms" of my own life.

—**CATHERINE ABBEY HODGES,** author of *Empty Me Full*

Those of us who have read and admired Paul Willis's poetry for many years tend to think of him as a writer most at home in the natural world. What a surprise, therefore, to see he is equally skilled at bringing to life the Italian town of Orvieto, its houses of worship, and its spectacular works of art. And yet, while they have been transported to Umbria, Willis's new poems retain the qualities of his earlier work: an unmatched eye for detail, gentle humor, soaring spirituality, and a fierce kindness that embraces the living and the dead, the sinning and those sinned against.

—**DAVID STARKEY,** author of *You, Caravaggio*

Paul Willis takes the reader on an intimate tour through vineyards and city streets, churches and tombs, and bridges that bear the memory of bombardiers—a memory that is alien to "orange and ochre butterflies." Far stronger than the pain of history is the mercy of "vineyards harvested of many grapes" and of "teal-gray streams," their current inviting us to a new year. And how could we not go, into and through this inspired and inspiring travelogue!

—**SOFIA M. STARNES,** author of *The Consequence of Moonlight*

Orvieto is not another poetic travelogue. Rather, it is a lyric and candid translation of the experience of place as it connects to history in general as well as personal history. It engages the political and the personal with humor, irony, and a keen poetic appreciation of the everyday, and the concentrated images and narrative transform specifics into the larger themes of our lives.

—**CHRISTOPHER BUCKLEY,** author of *Sprezzatura*

ORVIETO

Poems

PAUL J. WILLIS

ORVIETO

Paul J. Willis

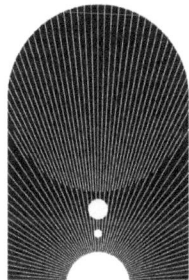

SOLUM
LITERARY PRESS

Anaheim, CA • solumpress.com

Solum Literary Press
2205 W Broadway A-119
Anaheim, CA 92804

solumpress.com

PAPERBACK ISBN 978-1-965169-09-4
EBOOK ISBN 978-1-965169-10-0

Cover art and design by Sarah Christolini.
Cover art inspired by the artwork of Matt Doll. https://matthew-doll.squarespace.com
Interior design by Riley Bounds.
Author photo by Brad Elliott. Used with permission.

LIBRARY OF CONGRESS CATALOGUING-IN-PUBLICATION DATA
Name: Willis, Paul, author.
Title: Orvieto / paul willis.
Description: Anaheim, CA: Solum Literary Press, 2025.
Identifiers: LCCN 2025943516
ISBN: 978-1-965169-09-4 (print)
ISBN: 978-1-965169-10-0 (Kindle)
Subjects: BISAC: POETRY / General / Subjects & Themes: Religious / Subjects & Themes: Places
LC record available at https://lccn.loc.gov/2025943516

for

Jeanne Murray Walker,

who got me there

Contents

ORVIETO

Shutters

In Orvieto, the cobblestone alleys
barely keep the walls apart,
the walls of tufa quarried from the cliffs

below. Doors and windows face
each other like next of kin
all into one another's business.

Across the way from my apartment,
a pair of fretted bird cages
hang in front of open shutters.

I thought such cages only existed
in old poems, yet here I am,
singing in one.

Sigmund Freud Slept Here

So says the bronze plaque
on the Corso Cavour.
But really? He just slept?

Freud being Freud, we
would expect something more.
An instance of incest, perhaps,

or some athletic fantasy
of the sexual imagination.
But even Freud needed to sleep.

All worn out, he needed a break
from the escapades of the flesh.
Sweet dreams, Sigmund Freud.

On the Way to Lake Bolsena

Under an oak by a quiet pasture,
away from the alleys of Orvieto,
the morning sun is welcome
on my arms and shoulders:
John Denver would be happy here.

Whether I am happy here or not
I haven't quite decided yet,
but a daylong walk in woods and fields
says to me that late October
is here as much as anywhere.

The pasture rolls to a verge of forest,
and beyond are the crimson,
vacant vines, rows of olive trees
in harvest, hazelnuts on a curving upland.
Even the blur of a wild boar.

And then, a lake in an old caldera,
larger than my circling spirits,
brighter than the afternoon.
Bolsena, you were good enough
for the Etruscans. And Romans, too.

Mark Twain compared each lake he met
to Tahoe in the far Sierra.
That's because he never saw Crater Lake
on the sky-blue crest of the Cascades.
But why compare? Why not

take each lake as it comes?
This one, for example, just over
the broad hill from a sunny pasture
ringed with oaks on the Via Romea,
lying in wait to take my hand.

Relief of a Roman Wedding

Museo Claudio Faina

Companions of the bride on our right,
groomsmen on the left. Not all of them
are paying attention (the best man looks off
into the distance, wondering when his turn
will come), but more solemn faces peek over
the shoulders of the starting line-up.

Beside the bride and groom in the center,
a special cluster of deities. Hymen, I think,
disrobed almost to the groin and holding up
his flaming tead. And a goddess of stature,
arms around the shoulders of the breathless pair,
her gaze turned toward the husband-to-be,
lips parted as if speaking holy instruction.
Could it be Venus, officiating? And beneath
and between the man and wife, a mostly nude
winged figure, legs missing. Cupid, perhaps?

The bride herself is missing both arms, cut off
at the elbow, but one hand reappears within
the solid grip of the groom. They look
with devotion at one another, he forthright
and curly-haired, she in a modest head scarf,
unlike the other women in braids and buns.

And off to the right of the bridesmaids,
a bearded man standing behind the full figure
of a bull. A sacrifice for the occasion?
For there is much to be sacrificed. But all this
company together—male and female, gods and friends
and kin and kine—they are still with us, are they not?
Always in witness, always about to be married,
ready to start what is not yet finished.

Etruscan of Pietra Campana

Museo Claudio Faina

Reclining in state, he looks out
from the lid of his sarcophagus
as if he has something to say.

The blunt projection of the nose,
the sure and certain pursing of lips,
the sheer directness of the gaze—

these suggest a confidence,
a long-accustomed authority
in his habits of speech.

But what's in the bowl upon his lap,
the one tipped slightly toward us
in the firm grip of his right hand?

Food for his walk to the underworld?
Red wine to pour along the path?
Coins for the gatekeeper of shadows?

And the rippled robe that reaches
from beneath his belly to the very tops
of his feet—does it keep him warm

in the afterlife? Is it merely for modesty?
If you look up *sarcophagus*
in the dictionary, you will find that it means,

in the Greek, "flesh-eating stone."
His body has now been consumed.
Yet his dignity—it lasts, it lasts.

Etruscan Tomb

Necropoli del Crocifisso del Tufo

A cold stone room with a low, peaked roof.
From the narrow entrance, ferns and lichen
trail the walls and floor within a stream of light.

Bless the gods for this bit of sun and greenery—
something that I could have used as I moldered
here among our coal-black Grecian urns.

But now there is a fluorescent tube
above the lintel—new since my time,
something to profane the night.

And why, after all these years, did they dig
us up again? Not that we were still here.
Just our slabs. Our bowls and rings and figurines—

bronze figurines of Hercules and our Menerva,
Bellerophon and Pegasus. Women in long chiton robes,
offering their pomegranates, men as naked as the sea.

They are yours now. Take them. Enjoy them.
Enjoy their neat arrangement on the many shelves
of your museums. And rest in peace.

Etruscan Tomb (II)

Necropoli del Crocifisso del Tufo

There is lettering over the lintel,
some of the characters fallen away
with the stone facing. The Etruscan
alphabet is remarkably like our own,
though the language itself, I am told,
has yet to be fully deciphered.

Here I see a crooked *S* and a top-heavy *A*,
followed by a barely recognizable *M*.
Let's call the former occupant Sam, then—
Etruscan Sam from the sixth century BC.

Farther on in the inscription, a backwards *D*,
little bow without an arrow, a letter
that looks like the lateral half of a fir tree,
and a *T* with a slanted roof,
unlike the roof of this tomb, perfectly
squared with blocks of tufa.

The rock is rougher than sandstone,
more like the compressed volcanic ash
that it is. Tan in color, as usual,
except when covered in moss or lichen
or bathed in darkness
within the rectangular chamber itself.

Two days ago, while walking the Percorso Rupe
beneath the cliffs of Orvieto (or Velzna,
as it was called), I found the opening
to a cave that was not, like the others,
completely blocked off by a gate.

So I went in, past bottles and scrap,
and followed a passage with the help
of the flashlight on my iPhone.
The roof was high and curved and chipped,
then suddenly low, and the way swung right,
then left, and concluded in the small womb
of a cul-de-sac. Then I took another branch
past square stone archways to where the passage
was filled by a cave-in from the side.

I thought of trying other ways, through
those empty doors of stone, but feared
I would end up like Tom Sawyer
and Becky Thatcher, lost with the threat
of some Etruscan Injun Joe, waiting
in ambush in the dark. Sudden Sam.

But those Etruscans are gone now,
and even their clustered tombs
are empty with only a few curious letters,
some of them much like our own,
etched above the square stone
doors we dare not enter,
lest we meet our former selves.

Twelve Stops on the Percorso Rupe

Are you a carrot-top or a fern,
growing here at the foot of the cliff?
Lace upon lace of branching green,
you wave *buon giorno* like a stranger.

*

This racy fence accompanies us
beside the trail, *XXX* along the way—
until one wooden *X* goes missing.
No matter, *XOX* may be more like it.

*

Racemes of fuchsia flowers,
tipped with a speckling of dark blue berries,
what a surprise
to see you here in November shade.

*

Smitty loves Asith—or so it would seem,
given the number of hearts on this napkin.
Three next to Smitty, five next to Asith—
who loves whom the most?

*

Hello? Hello? A broken box of telephone lines
is plugged into the side of the rock.
Inside, a nest of twigs—
a little desk for the operator.

*

That ivy-covered locust tree doesn't stand a chance
of growing straight and tall. It bends its back
above the path as if it bears the weight
of every free-loading cousin in town.

*

Are you just a gutter by the trail?
If so, you are one on a Roman scale,
those shelving blocks
another era gone down the drain.

*

This chestnut on the slippery stone is not yet out
of its half-split casing, which, unlike the others,
is still bright green—and spiny as a saltwater urchin.
Deep inside, the dark curve of a curious eye.

*

Trail blaze,
white stripe on red upon the rock,
why are you almost never there
at a fork in the way?

*

From our path in shadow, fields of sunlight
appear to the north and east, framed
by pillars of blackberry vines.
We didn't know it was a picture until we saw it.

*

Solar panel on a pole, why are you
in the umbrage of this golden tree?
Your one black wire seems to connect to exactly nothing,
another light bulb gone missing with the Etruscans.

*

PERCORSO RUP says the wooden sign—
all the letters it has left in the drip-drip-drip
of a shroud of ivy that reaches
up and up the cliff, into the clouds.

Simeon in the Temple

after a painting in the Church of Santa Maria dei Servi

Simeon, that's a big boy you've got on your hands.
He looks more like forty months than forty days.
He also looks like he knows what you are going
to say, and is just waiting for you to say it.
As in, *Come on, old man. Get on with the prophecy.*

It's hard to ignore that kind of impatience.
Makes you hesitate a little. Those sad and ancient
eyes of yours—all these years of waiting to offer
your pregnant part, and now to be upstaged
by a little god who just wants you to finish up.

So, maybe it is time to revise. Say something
a bit different than what you have long intended.
Promise a little pain ahead, a speaking against.
Falling and risings. Swords. Piercings.
For, why not? It's probably coming anyway.

15

Reliquary

del Beato Bonaventura Bonaccorsi

The golden casket lies inside a cage
behind a sword-pierced statue
of the sorrowing Virgin Mary.

It is low to the floor; I sit down
on a cold step of brick and marble
to peer through the glass sides.

At first I spy a simple bed of scattered
blossoms, white and pink, but then I see
that the flowers cover, on a pillow,

a pair of crossed and yellowed bones.
I don't aspire to end up parceled out
like that, but as I think about this friar

of long ago, a maker of peace
between contentious city-states,
I don't resent the effort to preserve

what little is left of him. And if
a breath of his fine dust might pacify
our lust for blood—well, let it.

Though swords still slash the Blessed Virgin,
at her feet there yet remains
a hidden balm of bones and blossoms.

In the Church of Santa Maria dei Servi

Halfway up one wall, a statue of Jesus
stands behind a glass door as if
he were a piece of china on display.
In fact, at his feet there is something like
a crimson dish—a medallion, maybe—
with a white heart at the center.
He wears a red robe over a snowy
tunic, and his right hand is extended
downward in a helpful sort of way
while his left hand is comfortably raised,
index finger pointing vaguely across his chest.

He looks down at us with a mild expression—
inviting, yes, but also sad and mysterious—
we don't quite know what he is thinking.
And his locks and beard are a little bit gray,
as if he were tired of waiting for us.
We know it is Jesus, though, because he
is wearing a spoked halo as big and strong
as a steering wheel on a UPS delivery truck.
Which means he has something to deliver.

And this is why they should let him out
of his crystalline closet. It's time, Jesus.
You can come down now, stretch your legs,
walk on out the door of the church
and catch some rays of morning sun
on the Piazza Belisario. Maybe even turn

the corner onto the Corso Cavour
and order a cone of chocolate gelato,
if the shop is open today. Then we can sit
at an iron table and catch you up
on all the gossip you have missed.
And you'll reach out with that hand
of yours and ask, beatifically,
Where did you say the napkins were?

In the Church of Sant'Andrea

Twelve stone steps rise to the pulpit,
wrapping around a granite column
beside a crooked banister.
On the column are ragged remains
of a crude fresco in red and black.
And among the figures in the fresco,
a sharp-eyed woman, robed and hooded,
looks down (then up) at the holy priest
as he ascends—as if to say,
Watch your words. I'm listening.
On other days, however, she says,
Don't worry. You can do this.

In the pulpit the preacher stands
some fourteen feet above
the heads of the congregation,
speaking to them from on high.
He might as well be Juliet
on her balcony. And maybe,
on his better days, he expresses his love
for them as Juliet to her Romeo.

But the one he longs for is behind him,
painted on the side of the column,
nodding at his every phrase. After
the homily is done, on his way
down those twelve stone steps,
he kisses the fingers of his hand
and places them on her fading lips.

Fresco Behind a Wooden Statue of Saint Andrew

On the plastered wall of the sanctuary of Sant'Andrea in Orvieto,
a strong young man in a green robe, red sleeves beneath, holds up
a bloody sword. As in so many frescoes of the Renaissance, his eyes
and nose and mouth have been dissolved by time. He is facing (if
you can call it facing) a red-robed woman on his right. Her eyes are
exceedingly sharp. She gestures toward him with one hand—a tight
gesture—and holds the other over her heart. The man, likewise, has
placed his left hand, loosely, over his own heart.

Behind him, and to his left, an older couple lie tucked in bed, face-
up. Their heads rest on matching pillows. The older man has a white
beard, neatly trimmed, and he wears a green night cap that matches
the young man's robe in color. The older woman wears a white head
scarf, just like the woman who is standing. The eyes of the couple
in bed are closed. Both of them are bleeding profusely from stab
wounds in the neck.

If it were not in a church, and if Duncan had a wife in the play, the
fresco would seem to mark the moment in which Macbeth says, *I
have done the deed*, the moment in which Lady Macbeth receives
the news in a fury of cold agitation. But this must be the story of the
martyrdom of some saint—of two saints. Mr. and Mrs. Saint. But
what if the two are not married? What if the woman in red is the wife
and the woman in bed is the paramour, the man in green the hired
assassin?

I wish we could see the swordsman's face. Is he aghast at what he has
done? Relieved to have taken vengeance? Simply glad to receive his
pay? St. Andrew might know, but his wooden statue has turned its
back on all this sorry business.

We have to look farther afield, to the crucifix above the altar. The very sad man hanging there, his face quite clear in its agonies, looks out across the nave and sees. And bleeds. And sees. And bleeds. And knows. And what he knows is that the faceless man with the sword is the one who will become a saint. Saint Julian. He has just murdered his own parents, who had come on a surprise visit while he was hunting, and who were sleeping in his bed when he came back. He has just murdered them because he thought he had found his wife cheating on him. But now his wife arrives to tell him he was mistaken, he was wrong, and Julian is filled with remorse. This is what the hanging man on the cross well knows. And he knows that Julian—and his wife, as well—will spend the rest of their stricken lives helping the sick and giving shelter to the weary. For a night of killing, years of care. And at once and at last, Julian will be forgiven. No longer seen in a fresco darkly, he will be known, and he will know. He will receive his face.

Angel

Well before dawn, awake in my bed,
shoulder throbbing, arm in a sling,
I thought of an angel at the entrance
to the Church of Santa Maria dei Servi
in Orvieto. The angel is part of a fresco
painting inside the main door and to the right,
in a little side chamber that is usually barred
and locked. Late one night, however,
I found the gate ajar, and entered.
And there on the wall was a sacred scene,
the exaltation of a saint or a day in the life
of the Virgin Mary, with attendant angels
looking on. Except one angel was looking right
out of the wall at me instead. At me, I swear,
with a gaze so direct and severe and knowing
and yet so welcoming as well, straight out
of the Renaissance. There was something pure
about those eyes, and eternally young, and full
of holy energy. And I felt seen, and I
felt known, and I felt transfixed and included,
with or without my will. That is what
I knew that night, and this night too,
though my aching shoulder still throbbed,
and I lay sleepless, and it seemed the pain
would never end.

Saint Francis in Ecstasy

after Caravaggio

The angel looks tenderly interested—
uncommonly so—in the sacked-out figure
of Francis gently supported in his arms.

Or maybe he is just patiently waiting
for this mortal to wake from his spiritual coma
so that he can depart on yet another appointed round—

rescuing the next pope from his cardinal sins
or plucking a child from a deep canal
outside a doorstep in Venice.

In any case, Francis' dark-haired, bearded head
lolls back in the swaddled lap of the divine messenger,
who in this instance has nothing to say,

Francis being, as he is, beyond sight or hearing
or sensation. And that rough brown robe of the earthy
saint, tied at the waist with a simple cord,

must be scratching those perfectly formed angelic thighs
in a most uncomfortable way. Forbearance,
though, is a heavenly virtue which shines in the light

like the bare shoulder of this visitor with the exquisite
bedside manner—the same shoulder that somehow sprouts,
from the back of the scapula, a dusky wing.

Dear Francis

Rick Steves says you are the guy with the sunroof haircut.
Do I know much more about you than that? Father Larry,
my friend back home in Santa Barbara who goes
around in a rough brown robe and leather sandals,
he's a Franciscan just like you, though eight hundred years
after your act. Father Larry has a plump, round face,
red as a delicious apple, and always seems to be bobbing
and smiling as people try to impress him with the things
they've done, trying to make up for what they've told him
in the confessional. He writes poems and includes
them in his homilies, which he sends me every month or so,
because I am Protestant and not in attendance at the Mission,
the landmark of our little town. The poems are not quite
up to par with your canticles (whose are?) but his sermons
have a certain gracious lilt about them. And once,
during our Hiroshima Remembrance Day, Father Larry
held forth powerfully with the words of the weeping
prophet, Jeremiah, which made me think of that stone
pulpit in the vast basilica built over your tomb, Francis,
and the frescoes painted by Giotto of you earnestly
holding forth to larks, to monks, to the pope, even—
for yours became a preaching order. Do we have you to blame,
then, for the forty-minute sermons in my Evangelical church
that could easily be compressed within the space of an egg timer?
But maybe your sermons were memorable at any length,
filled with heart-deep eloquence and earthy wisdom.
(Would the birds have settled for anything less?)

And when I visited your crypt, there was a young man
holding on to the iron grating around your bones
and leaning his head against those bars with eyes shut tight
and tears staining his sallow cheeks. I felt bad
to be just a tourist in the presence of such clear devotion.
I pray now that you would make me—and by *you* I mean
your supposed example—that you would make me
more than a tourist, at least for a day. Kiss me, Francis.
If you can.

Confessional

Now we have therapists with whom we sit
face-to-face in soft chairs, not screened off
in coffined booths, the priest hunching on a bench
in curtained gloom, the penitent kneeling
just outside, gripping the wooden lintel in fear.

And yet, maybe they had it right.
Is it easier to tell dark secrets in the dark,
on aching knees? Does something—
even everything—remain hidden in the glow
of a faux living room, lattes in hand?

In either case, at least we can honor the delicate
task of discernment in the ones who listen
in light and in dark—their recognition of honest
trembling on the threshold, the shaking
of the hand on the cup. The wise priests
of any era have their work cut out for them.
Drawing the curtain. Piercing the soul.

The Fortune Teller

after Caravaggio

The woman reading the young man's palm
looks caring and innocent enough—
ordinary, even, in her wrapped cloth cap
and white bloused sleeves, overlain
with a plain dark dress. In another life,
maybe her own, she would be out
milking the cows instead of cupping
this fellow's hand in a motherly way
while grazing the inside of his fingers,
especially his ring finger, with the feathering
tips of her own.
                    She returns his gaze
as if trying to decide whether and how
to break the news of the future to such
a trusting soul—also mindful that he
is somewhat richly dressed in a gold coat
edged with black, and that he does have
his other hand near the ornate hilt
of his sword.
                    But his face is much too
pudgy and self-satisfied for his own good,
and that ostrich feather in his cap
bespeaks misplaced pride. No telling,
in this moment, what will become
of that hint of fear within his eyes.
In the end, fine fortune or no,
his gaudy ring will be gone, and he
may be the wiser for it. And she,
the teller of this tale, will be touching
upon her next story.

A Statue of Pope Boniface VIII, Sculpted in AD 1297, That Once Sat over the Porta Maggiore

Museo Claudio Faina

Weathered you are from all those years poised atop
the gate of the city. Yet robed, of course, in mottled
marble, and sporting a tall miter that, eroded by time,
looks more like a dunce cap—with an iron piton hook
behind to keep you from doing a Humpty Dumpty.

Your ears are tucked almost in the back of your head,
unwilling to hear the words of Dante. Your nose
flattened, eyes erased but still downcast as if in prayer—
or, more likely, as if inspecting with suspicion all who walk
beneath your gaze. And your lips, gone now, are sealed—

nothing left to curse or to bless. *Boniface* means
not "good face," as I once supposed, but "good fate."
Forgive me, Father, when I say your destiny
has been more or less like that of all your fellow
travelers, all who pass beyond that gate.

World War I Memorial

a tutti caduti per la patria

Three figures bent in agony,
shielding their helmets with their hands.
Atop, an angel, holding a wreath up to the sky.

Behind, the names of local men who lost
their lives in the cold of the Alps,
the wet of the trenches of France.

The clouds sail past, hiding and releasing
a November sun. A man in a green sweatshirt
appends a plaque to the unknown soldier,

milite ignoto, a hundred years after the fact.
Below the walls and cliffs of the city,
the golden rows of empty vines.

A Birthday Abroad

The man was lost in Italy, where he
had gone to teach a class in poetry—
not lost, exactly, though at times he walked
the country lanes and paused in wonder, balked
by lack of understanding of the way.
His birthday came—his sixty-sixth—a stay.
Except, he did not tell his students this;
to focus on himself would be amiss
he felt, and so he kept his frigid room
and greeted all his family on Zoom.
The day before, at midnight, came a storm
of thunder and of lightning—not the norm,
his students told him. Afterward he hiked
to where a butte of tufa lava spiked
the north horizon. On the very top,
a dripping forest spread its verdant mop,
and at its side a quiet chapel grew
as if it were a piece of forest too.
Inside, a spectral silence whispered what
he could not hear: *The years! The years!* A nut
of hazel rolled across the empty floor.
He stood and watched it, pausing in the door.
And then he fled through many a muddy field,
through crimson vineyards past their sparkling yield
of months ago, the grapes and wine all past,
and living in the lees of life at last.

Allerona Bridge

All is confusion when the river comes.
The unexploded bombs appear again,
unearthed from out their graves. It is as if
the flood returns them, dropping from the sky,
the way they did that day in January
when Allied planes from Sicily amassed
above the bridge, assigned to interrupt
the rail supply to Nazi troops along
the heavily defended Winter Line.
There was a train stalled on the span that day—
a bonus target. Bombardiers let fly
shell after shell upon the reeling cars.
But what they did not know was, locked inside,
eight hundred prisoners from South Africa,
America, and England took the brunt
of those explosions, perishing en masse.
The few that found their way out from the wreck
were forced to choose: flee barefoot (for their boots
were in the hands of German captors) or
remain to tend the wounded in their gore.
The pilots and their crews did not find out
till later what they'd done. The train had not
been marked with crosses as it should have been—
no matter, they still bore the smart of all
that suffering they had unleashed upon
the men caged in those cars. They took the guilt
to their own graves. (And there were those who wished
they had been shot down from the clouds and died
in ignorance of their complicity.)

But when that river floods, the Paglia,
to this day sleeping ordnance awakes,
comes lurching to the shore like sightless men.
The highway and the rail line then are closed,
live arteries from Florence slowed and stilled,
and teams of specialists approach with fear,
unable, finally, to defuse the past.

On the Monument to the Murdered Seven

I didn't know the story at first. I had assumed that because of the date on the monument, 1944, this curious figure full of hollows, arms raised high, was placed beneath umbrella pines atop the cliffs to celebrate the liberation of the city. But the plaque says March, and the city wasn't freed until June, another tale altogether—how the Nazi commander, so in love with the golden facade of the Duomo, visible for miles around, relinquished the town to the British without firing a single gun. They say he had become friends with the bishop, locked himself inside the cathedral for private recitals on the organ. *We'll fight elsewhere*, he said. And they did.

But this same Nazi commander, three months earlier, because of some small act of resistance, chose at random seven young men of the city to be taken below the walls and shot. And that is the moment, not of relief but of lasting shock, which is recalled in this stone statue full of space.

Federico, Raimondo, Raimondo, Alberto, Duilo, Amore, Ulderico.

I nostri cari.

Two of Us

Italian graveyards come complete with photographs
of the departed. Take this one, in black-and-white,
of a man and wife who are not smiling for the camera.

Why should they, when they know they will end up here
beneath rows of cypress? Her dark hair is combed flat
against her skull, and she stands shoulder-to-shoulder
with her husband, he of the high-collared uniform,

the pencil-thin black mustache, the shako cap
with the narrow brim. On the front of the cap is the white
shape of a bird of prey and the bald number 87.

The more important number, though, is the date
of his death, 1944, that year of Nazi boots and guns
(whichever side he may have been on).

Her date of departure is 1979, marking her as a lone
widow for thirty-five years. Reunited, they stare
at us impassively, no secrets told, as if to say,
Travelers, we are none of your damn business.

On the Via Romea, in November

Steep, muddy trail slides
  down from Rocca Ripésena
    to a quick pair of teal-gray streams
      joining under a slippery log.

Hazelnut, maple, cottonwood
  contribute their gold coins
    to the current, sending
      last wishes for a new year.

Vineyard Below Castel Rubello

Now, in November, the vineyard has long
been harvested of its many grapes. The vines
relax themselves in the sun and drop lazy leaves,
gold and crimson, onto the long green paths.

Row on row bends down the slope in careless
flame until lost in shadow below the castle on the hill,
a place contested by Dante's Guelphs and Ghibellines,
then later damaged—two of the towers—in the
Second World War. Orange and ochre butterflies

traverse the air around my knees, and a pale gentian
blooms alone beside my boots. If you asked them
about blood betrayals and flying shells of artillery,
they wouldn't know. They absolutely wouldn't know.

Acknowledgments

I want to thank Matt Doll, director of the Gordon-in-Orvieto program, for including me on his teaching staff in the fall of 2021 and the fall of 2024. All of the poems in this chapbook found their origin in those month-long visits to Italy.

I am also grateful to the editors of the following journals in which some of these poems first appeared, sometimes in different versions:

Abandoned Mine: "Sigmund Freud Slept Here"

Amethyst: "Fresco Behind a Wooden Statue of Saint Andrew" and "Saint Francis in Ecstasy"

Christian Century: "Angel," "In the Church of Sant'Andrea," and "Reliquary"

Curator: "Simeon in the Temple"

SALT: "In the Church of Santa Maria dei Servi," "On the Monument to the Murdered Seven," "On the Via Romea, in November," "Shutters," and "World War I Memorial"

Southern Poetry Review: "Etruscan of Pietra Campana"

Triggerfish Critical Review: "Two of Us"

Turtle Island Quarterly: "Vineyard Below Castel Rubello"

www.ingramcontent.com/pod-product-compliance
Lightning Source LLC
Chambersburg PA
CBHW030815090426
42737CB00010B/1281